STARK COUNTY DISTRICT LIBRARY

SEQUENCING STORIES

Making Lemonade

MEG GAERTNER

Published by The Child's World®
1980 Lookout Drive • Mankato, MN 56003-1705
800-599-READ • www.childsworld.com

Photographs ©: Antonio Diaz/Shutterstock Images, cover (left), cover (middle right), cover (right), 3 (left), 5, 9, 13, 14, 17, 18, 21; iStockphoto, cover (middle left); Shutterstock Images, 3 (right), 6, 10

Copyright © 2020 by The Child's World®
All rights reserved. No part of this book may be reproduced or utilized in any form or by any means without written permission from the publisher.

ISBN 9781503835085
LCCN 2018963174

Printed in the United States of America
PA02425

About the Author

Meg Gaertner is a children's book author and editor who lives in Minnesota. When not writing, she enjoys dancing and spending time outdoors.

CONTENTS

Summertime! . . . 4

Glossary . . . 22
To Learn More . . . 23
Index . . . 24

Summertime!

It is summer! The sun shines all of the time. The days are hot and long. Sophie wants to celebrate. She will make lemonade with her mom today.

What do you like to do in summer?

You can make lemonade with fresh-squeezed lemon juice, bottled juice, or lemonade mix.

First, Sophie gathers all of the **ingredients**. She needs lemons, sugar, and water to make lemonade. Meanwhile, her mom grabs a **pitcher**, a knife, and a **juicer**.

Next, Sophie's mom cuts the lemons in half. She cuts on a cutting board. This is so she does not damage the counter.

Fun Fact
Roll lemons on the counter before cutting them. This helps release the lemon juice.

Kids should let an adult help when using knives.

Lemon juice is very tart.

Then it is Sophie's turn to work. She takes a lemon half. She presses the juicer into it. She presses down hard. She uses a bowl to collect all of the lemon juice.

By now the lemon juice is ready. Sophie adds the juice to the pitcher of water. Then she squeezes a bit more lemon juice by hand. She likes her lemonade extra **tart**!

Do you like any tart foods or drinks?

Like lemonade, people make limeade with limes.

While Sophie adds the juice, her mom cuts up more slices of lemon. She drops these slices into the pitcher.

Finally it is time to add the sugar.

Sophie drops in one spoonful of sugar.

Right away she adds another.

She stirs the lemonade and tastes it. It is a bit too tart!

Fun Fact

Some **recipes** say to cook the sugar in water on the stove first. Then you let the sugar water cool.

Cooks try the food as they prepare it so it tastes good.

Sometimes people make pink lemonade. It is regular lemonade that has a pink color.

Immediately, Sophie adds a few more spoonfuls of sugar. She stirs the lemonade. Her mother pours them each a glass.

It is delicious! The lemonade is the perfect mix of sweet and tart. It tastes great on a hot summer day.

Fun Fact

Sometimes people create a lemonade stand. They sell cups of lemonade on the side of the road.

Have you ever made lemonade?

Glossary

ingredients (in-GREE-dee-uhnts) Ingredients are items that something else is made from. Sugar and lemons are two ingredients in lemonade.

juicer (JOOS-ur) A juicer is a tool used to squeeze out the juice of fruits. Sophie used a juicer to get lemon juice.

pitcher (PICH-ur) A pitcher is a container for liquids that has an open top and a lip for pouring. Sophie mixed all her lemonade ingredients in a pitcher.

recipes (RESS-i-pees) Recipes are instructions for making meals or drinks. There are many recipes for making lemonade.

tart (TART) Something that is tart tastes sour or sharp. Sophie added sugar to make the lemonade less tart.

To Learn More

BOOKS

D'Alessandro, Cathy, and Noelle Hoffmeister. *Money Matters: The Lemonade Stand*. Huntington Beach, CA: Teacher Created Materials, 2018.

Spalding, Maddie. *Weather in Summer*. Mankato, MN: The Child's World, 2018.

WEBSITES

Visit our website for links about making lemonade:
childsworld.com/links

Note to Parents, Teachers, and Librarians: We routinely verify our Web links to make sure they are safe and active sites. So encourage your readers to check them out!

Index

ingredients, 7

juicer, 7, 11

lemon, 7–8, 11–12, 15
lemon juice, 8, 11–12

pitcher, 7, 12, 15

sugar, 7, 16, 19
summer, 4, 20

tart, 12, 16, 20

water, 7, 12, 16

3 1333 04852 1775